The Wonder of
BLACK BEARS

Adapted from Jeff Fair's *Black Bear Magic for Kids*
by Beth Karpfinger
Photography by Flip Nicklin

Gareth Stevens Publishing
MILWAUKEE

For a free color catalog describing Gareth Stevens' list of high-quality books, call 1-800-341-3569 (USA) or 1-800-461-9120 (Canada).

Library of Congress Cataloging-in-Publication Data

Karpfinger, Beth.
    The wonder of black bears / adapted from Jeff Fair's Black bear magic for kids by Beth Karpfinger ;
photography by Lynn Rogers.
       p. cm. — (Animal wonders)
    Includes index.
    Summary: Text and photographs introduce a creature of the North American forest, the black bear.
    ISBN 0-8368-0855-X
    1. Black bear—Juvenile literature. [1. Black bear. 2. Bears.] I. Rogers, Lynn L., ill. II. Fair, Jeff. Black
bear magic for kids. III. Title. IV. Series.
    QL737.C27K365   1992
    599.74'446—dc20   92-16944

North American edition first published in 1992 by
Gareth Stevens Publishing
1555 North RiverCenter Drive, Suite 201
Milwaukee, WI 53212, USA

This U.S. edition is abridged from *Black Bear Magic for Kids,* copyright © 1991 by NorthWord Press, Inc.,
and written by Jeff Fair, first published in 1991 by NorthWord Press, Inc., and published in a library
edition by Gareth Stevens, Inc., in 1991. Additional end matter copyright © 1992 by Gareth Stevens, Inc.

Cover design: Kristi Ludwig

Printed in the United States of America

1 2 3 4 5 6 7 8 9 98 97 96 95 94 93 92

Black bears and people
have a lot in common.
Bears have bodies that
remind us of our own.
They stand tall on their
back legs and make deep
tracks that look like
human footprints.

Black bears are large
mammals that live
only in North America.
They get their name from
their thick fur, which is
usually black.

We hunt them and destroy their forest home.

Female black bears may weigh as much as 300 pounds. Males may reach 500 pounds. The biggest black bear ever weighed was over 800 pounds! But even with all that weight, bears easily outrun humans.

Black bears can be found in the forests of North America.

Forests with nuts and acorns provide the best bear *habitat*.

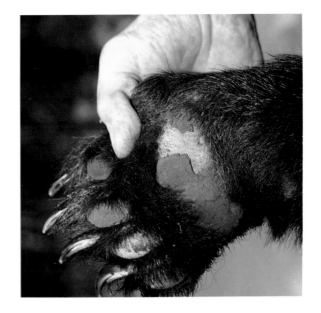

With their sharp, curved claws, black bears climb trees to find food and to escape things that scare them, such as people or larger bears.

Black bears are more frightened of us than we are of them! Even though they are not likely to hurt us, we should treat them with care. We should never feed them or walk up to them.

This man studies black
bears in their habitat.
The bears know he won't
hurt them.

He may spend an entire day and night with a bear family.

He records everything they eat and everything they do.

Black bears eat grasses, dandelions, and berries. They also eat leaves, wild-flowers, and nuts. Black bears may eat meat when it's easy to catch, but they are not very good *predators*. When they do catch *prey*, it's usually some kind of insect, such as ants, bees, or yellow jackets.

Late in the fall, the bears begin to slow down.

Soon they will begin a long, magical sleep. We call this sleep *hibernation*. Some bears hibernate in a hole between rocks, under a log, or high up in a hollow tree. Some bears hibernate right on top of the ground.

Hibernation allows bears to survive the winter when none of their foods are available. During hibernation, a bear's body slows down and uses less energy. The energy the bear does use comes from the fat it has stored from eating nuts last fall.

In spring, when the snow melts and the days grow longer, the black bears slowly awaken.

Spring is the harshest time for black bears. There is little food available, and they may still have to live off of their stored fat.

Black bear mothers give
birth to their young in
January, right in the
middle of hibernation.
The cubs are born tiny
and helpless.

By March, the cubs' eyes
are open, and their claws
are long and sharp. They
feel like puppies, but they
sound like baby humans.

When the cubs come out of their dens in the springtime,

they will weigh between four and eight pounds.

The *sow* takes good care of her cubs. She protects them, teaches them how to climb trees, and shows them which foods to eat.

When the cubs are two years old, they leave their mother. Now they are on their own.

People, not animals, are the biggest threat to bears.

We hunt them and destroy their forest home.

We often do not understand
that bears must be left
alone to live in the wild.

Long ago, native peoples of North America understood black bears. They shared the forest with black bears and other wild animals.

With a little understanding from us today, black bears will continue to thrive and remind us of the wonder of nature.

Glossary

habitat – the place where an animal or plant naturally lives and grows

hibernation – spending the winter in close quarters in a sleeplike condition

mammal – warm-blooded animal that has a backbone and usually has some hair or fur on its body

predator – an animal that lives by killing and eating other animals

prey – an animal hunted or caught by another animal for food

sow – an adult female bear; an adult male bear is called a boar

Index